UNPLUG

BREATHE

CREATE

A MONTH OF MAKING PEACE
WITH YOUR INNER SABOTEUR
THROUGH MEDITATION

Unplug Breathe Create: A Month of Making Peace With Your Inner Saboteur Through Meditation is a work of my own creation.

The information in this book was correct at the time of publication, and the Author does not assume any liability for loss or damage caused by errors or omissions, again, this is my perspective, opinion, and experience, so it has been written as such.

ISBN - 979-8-9870447-1-1

Cover, Book Design, and Layout by megs thompson, megswrites llc
www.megswrites.com

www.inomniaparatuspublishing.com

"IT'S NOT WHO YOU ARE THAT HOLDS YOU BACK, IT'S WHO YOU THINK YOU'RE NOT."

—DENIS WAITLEY

This journal is part of the
UNPLUG BREATHE CREATE
series & designed to be used
alongside a bespoke guided
meditation.

Download this month's meditation
using the QR code below:

HOW TO BEST USE THIS JOURNAL & MEDITATION

UNPLUG

The first step to reconnecting with ourselves as creative beings is to unplug & disconnect even temporarily from the countless electronic tethers that keep us firmly held in the world of shoulds & must's.

BREATHE

Take a few deep breaths, paying close attention to the way oxygen moves through your mouth & nose, filling your lungs & reawakening the creative genius locked safely within you, exhaling any fears, hesitations, or doubts that may filter your magic.

CREATE

Release your desire to control, plan & perfect every step & movement you make. Embrace the often wild, messy & chaotic magic that comes with allowing your inner creative to explore & play. Prepare yourself to experience fulfillment & satisfaction in new & creative ways.

DAILY ROUTINE

While moving through your day, begin implementing the use of affirmations. Both habits & beliefs are formed & strengthened through consistent repetition & before you know it your thoughts will become truths.

Included below are powerful affirmations that when paired with your daily tasks & activities, will empower you through this month of finding & claiming your own creative space.

I recommend repeating one or more of these affirmations aloud anytime you find yourself in front of a mirror, washing your hands, or refilling your beverage of choice.

MY CREATIVITY IS A SUPERPOWER.

I EXPRESS MYSELF WITH CREATIVITY & CONFIDENCE.

I FIND CLARITY & PEACE IN MY UNIQUE CREATIVE PROCESS.

30-DAY ENERGY TRACKER

When you've completed your daily meditation, make note of a single word or phrase that best describes your energy level in that moment.

Day 1	Day 2	Day 3	Day 4	Day 5
Day 6	Day 7	Day 8	Day 9	Day 10
Day 11	Day 12	Day 13	Day 14	Day 15
Day 16	Day 17	Day 18	Day 19	Day 20
Day 21	Day 22	Day 23	Day 24	Day 25
Day 26	Day 27	Day 28	Day 29	Day 30

DAY 1

When we're able to name our inner saboteur, it allows us to take back the power we've given it in the past. What name have you given your inner saboteur? Why? How does it feel, for them to have a name & no longer be an unknown stranger?

_____

_____

_____

_____

_____

_____

_____

_____

_____

_____

_____

_____

_____

_____

_____

_____

ON A SCALE OF 1-5 WHAT'S YOUR
CURRENT CREATIVITY LEVEL?

DAY 2

During meditation, you visualized your inner saboteur. Describe in detail how they appeared. Are they human, animal, celestial? Do they remind you of someone or something in your past? Do they speak? If so, how do they sound?

_____

_____

_____

_____

_____

_____

_____

_____

_____

_____

_____

_____

_____

_____

_____

ON A SCALE OF 1-5 WHAT'S YOUR
CURRENT CREATIVITY LEVEL?

DAY 3

Now that you've have a clear idea of what your inner saboteur looks & sounds like, and have given them a name, it's time to give them a story. Where are they from? Were they born, hatched, spawned, or did they simply 'poof' into existence? What are their hobbies? Their likes, dislikes, life purpose? How would you describe their personality?

_____

_____

_____

_____

_____

_____

_____

_____

_____

_____

_____

_____

_____

_____

_____

ON A SCALE OF 1-5 WHAT'S YOUR
CURRENT CREATIVITY LEVEL?

DAY 4

What traits or attributes do you recognize within you inner saboteur, that you also possess yourself? Are these traits you admire or dislike?

ON A SCALE OF 1-5 WHAT'S YOUR
CURRENT CREATIVITY LEVEL?

DAY 5

Write a letter to your inner saboteur, your ego,
thanking them to protecting you from harm &
releasing them from their role, expressing the
confidence you have in being creatively vulnerable.
You know now that your creativity is a superpower,
not a weakness.

ON A SCALE OF 1-5 WHAT'S YOUR
CURRENT CREATIVITY LEVEL?

DAY 6

When have you noticed your inner saboteur is most present? Are there specific situations, experiences, emotions, thoughts, or people that tend to waken them?

ON A SCALE OF 1-5 WHAT'S YOUR CURRENT CREATIVITY LEVEL?

DAY 7

t's important to recognize that our inner saboteur is a part of ourselves, not an enemy to be fought against. Often times they're formed from the assumptions, expectations, or perceived shortcomings that we adopt from others. Make a list of the negative self-talk your inner saboteur whispers in your ear - recognizing as you do, which are true & which are not.

ON A SCALE OF 1-5 WHAT'S YOUR
CURRENT CREATIVITY LEVEL?

DAY 8

Using the list you created yesterday, make a new list of the truths about who you are, what you do, and the power of your unique creative genius. For example; instead of referring to yourself as a perfectionist, you may see yourself as having great attention to detail.

ON A SCALE OF 1-5 WHAT'S YOUR
CURRENT CREATIVITY LEVEL?

DAY 9

When do you first remember being away of your inner saboteur? What do you remember about that experience or encounter? What were you doing? Feeling? Thinking?

_____

_____

_____

_____

_____

_____

_____

_____

_____

_____

_____

_____

_____

_____

_____

_____

_____

ON A SCALE OF 1-5 WHAT'S YOUR
CURRENT CREATIVITY LEVEL?

DAY 10

Close your eyes. Take 3 deep breaths & ask yourself, how do I want to explore my creativity today? What answer do you receive? How comfortable are you with trusting your intuition to guide your creativity?

_____

_____

_____

_____

_____

_____

_____

_____

_____

_____

_____

_____

_____

_____

_____

_____

ON A SCALE OF 1-5 WHAT'S YOUR
CURRENT CREATIVITY LEVEL?

DAY 11

When was the last time you created something for fun, without purpose or direction? Write a brief note to your inner saboteur letting them know how this experience felt. What you enjoyed most about the process. What hesitations you may have experienced. End your note by assuring them that you survived the experience & intend to do so again!

ON A SCALE OF 1-5 WHAT'S YOUR
CURRENT CREATIVITY LEVEL?

DAY 12

What is one creative outlet, modality, or experiment that you've wanted to try in the past but haven't? What's stopped you in the past? What needs to happen in order for you to make this dream a reality?

ON A SCALE OF 1-5 WHAT'S YOUR
CURRENT CREATIVITY LEVEL?

DAY 13

Where do you feel most creative? Is it a specific room, a place outdoors, a hidden getaway? Describe this place or space using all of your senses, in as much detail as possible.

DAY 14

Who do you consider to be the most creative person you know? What is it about them that makes you feel this way? Are these attributes or traits things they've learned, or are they innately natural?

_____

_____

_____

_____

_____

_____

_____

_____

_____

_____

_____

_____

_____

_____

_____

_____

_____

ON A SCALE OF 1-5 WHAT'S YOUR
CURRENT CREATIVITY LEVEL?

DAY 15

Make a list of ways that you can move outside of your comfort zone, to explore your own creative genius. These may be small, such as working from a different area of your home, or larger, such as hiring a coach to help you write & publish your first book. Once you have a list, choose one option & jot down the steps necessary to make this happen & get it on the calendar!

ON A SCALE OF 1-5 WHAT'S YOUR
CURRENT CREATIVITY LEVEL?

DAY 16

Failure is a part of life, it's also part of the creative process. When did you last fail during a creative project? Focus on the fact that while the outcome may have fallen short of your intention, it was temporary & there is no reason to not try again.

ON A SCALE OF 1-5 WHAT'S YOUR
CURRENT CREATIVITY LEVEL?

DAY 17

How often do you allow yourself to embrace your own creativity? What's holding you back from prioritizing this time? As with any habit or skill, consistent repetition strengthens & solidifies your confidence as a creative being. Are you able to set aside 10, 20, or even 30 minutes each day to explore your creativity?

ON A SCALE OF 1-5 WHAT'S YOUR
CURRENT CREATIVITY LEVEL?

DAY 18

What are 3 traits that set you apart from others?
Think of things that make you the unique individual
you are. How do these attributes serve you? How do
they limit you?

ON A SCALE OF 1-5 WHAT'S YOUR
CURRENT CREATIVITY LEVEL?

DAY 19

What are your favorite methods of self care? When was the last time you set aside time to take care of yourself? It's important that we show appreciation to our minds, bodies, hearts & souls - for carrying us through life. This also shows love to our inner saboteur, recognizing & showing gratitude for the ways in which they've protected us in the past.

ON A SCALE OF 1-5 WHAT'S YOUR
CURRENT CREATIVITY LEVEL?

DAY 20

What's your personal superpower? If you aren't able to think of something, ask a friend or family member to share what they see as your superpower. How are you using this skill in your daily life?

ON A SCALE OF 1-5 WHAT'S YOUR
CURRENT CREATIVITY LEVEL?

DAY 21

Write a letter of gratitude to yourself. Be proud of who you are, the things you've accomplished, and situations you've overcome.

_____

_____

_____

_____

_____

_____

_____

_____

_____

_____

_____

_____

_____

_____

_____

_____

ON A SCALE OF 1-5 WHAT'S YOUR
CURRENT CREATIVITY LEVEL?

DAY 22

What's one activity that cheers you up no matter what else might be going on? When was the last time you enjoyed this activity? What is it about the experience that you enjoy the most?

ON A SCALE OF 1-5 WHAT'S YOUR
CURRENT CREATIVITY LEVEL?

DAY 23

Where do you feel the most resistance when it comes
to embracing your own creativity? Are these feelings
based in past experiences or assumptions? What are
3 actions you can take, to soothe this resistance?

ON A SCALE OF 1-5 WHAT'S YOUR
CURRENT CREATIVITY LEVEL?

DAY 24

When do you feel the most creatively confident?

ON A SCALE OF 1-5 WHAT'S YOUR
CURRENT CREATIVITY LEVEL?

DAY 25

What forms of creative expression do you find come most easily, naturally, to you? When do remember first being aware of this ease? How might you apply these same feelings to new forms of creative expression?

_____

_____

_____

_____

_____

_____

_____

_____

_____

_____

_____

_____

_____

_____

_____

_____

_____

ON A SCALE OF 1-5 WHAT'S YOUR
CURRENT CREATIVITY LEVEL?

DAY 26

When was the last time you turned on a podcast or audiobook, busted out the colored pencils, pens, or crayons & gave yourself permission to spend an afternoon coloring?

ON A SCALE OF 1-5 WHAT'S YOUR
CURRENT CREATIVITY LEVEL?

DAY 27

How are you currently communicating your unique
voice, message, or story to others? How might you be
able to bring more creativity into this process? What
feelings or hesitations do you feel around this?

ON A SCALE OF 1-5 WHAT'S YOUR
CURRENT CREATIVITY LEVEL?

DAY 28

As children, we're naturally curious & willing to try new things, getting creative even when it may be uncomfortable. How can you embrace your childlike curiosity & creativity now?

_____

_____

_____

_____

_____

_____

_____

_____

_____

_____

_____

_____

_____

_____

ON A SCALE OF 1-5 WHAT'S YOUR
CURRENT CREATIVITY LEVEL?

DAY 29

Oftentimes the key to building creative confidence is maintaining a beginner's mindset, remaining open & curious to the countless solutions surrounding us. How can you better embrace a beginners mindset?

ON A SCALE OF 1-5 WHAT'S YOUR
CURRENT CREATIVITY LEVEL?

DAY 30

When do you feel most creatively confident? Where in your body do you feel this? How would you describe this feeling or sensation? How might you be able to weave this into your daily life?

_____

_____

_____

_____

_____

_____

_____

_____

_____

_____

_____

_____

_____

_____

_____

_____

_____

_____

ON A SCALE OF 1-5 WHAT'S YOUR
CURRENT CREATIVITY LEVEL?

If you already have an
UNPLUG BREATHE CREATE
subscription, keep an eye on your
mailbox for your next delivery.

If you aren't yet a member but
would like to be, or are
interested in gifting a
membership to someone else,
scan the QR code below.